CAPITAL LETTERS IN CURSIVE

AoBoCoDoEoFoGo

HoIoJoKoLoMoNo

OoPoQoRoSoTooUo

VoWoXoYoZo

Lowercase letters in cursive

aobocodoeofogohoo

iojokolomonoooo

poqorosotouovoo

woxoyozo

Be still, and know that I am **God**.

GodoGodoGodo

God God God

godogodogodo

god god god

Be still, and know that I am **God**.

GodoGodoGodo

God God God

godogodogodo

god god god

Be still, and know that I am **God**.

For we walk by **faith**, not by sight.

Fa i thooFaithoFaitho

Faith Faith Faith

faithofaithofaitho

faithofaithofaith

For we walk by **faith**, not by sight.

Fa i thooFaithoFaitho

Faith Faith Faith

faithofaithofaitho

faithofaithofaith

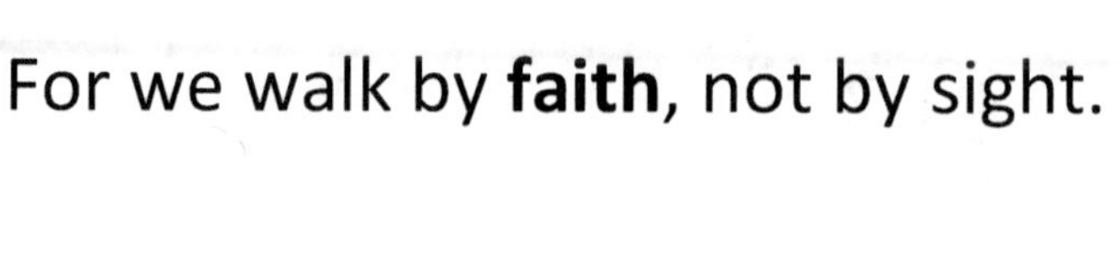

For we walk by **faith**, not by sight.

The **Lord** is my shepherd, I shall not want.

LordoLordoLordo

Lord Lord Lord

lordolordolordo

lord lord lord

The **Lord** is my shepherd, I shall not want.

LordoLordoLordo

Lord Lord Lord

lordolordolordo

lord lord lord

The **Lord** is my shepherd, I shall not want.

Bless them which persecute you, **bless**, and curse not.

BlessoBlessoBlesso

Bless Bless Bless

blessoblessoblesso

bless bless bless

Bless them which persecute you, **bless**, and curse not.

BlessoBlessoBlesso

Bless Bless Bless

blessoblessoblesso

bless bless bless

Bless them which persecute you, **bless**, and curse not.

I will **joy** in the God of my salvation.

JoyoJoyoJoyo

Joy Joy Joy

joyojoyojoyo

joy joy joy

I will **joy** in the God of my salvation.

JoyoJoyoJoyo

Joy Joy Joy

joyojoyojoyo

joy joy joy

I will **joy** in the God of my salvation.

I will **joy** in the God of my salvation.

Salvat i onoSalvationo

Salvation Salvation

salvat i onosalvationo

salvation salvation

I will **joy** in the God of my salvation.

Salvat i onoSalvationo

Salvation Salvation

salvat i onosalvationo

salvation salvation

I will **joy** in the God of my salvation.

Let there be **light**, and there was light.

LightoLightoLighto

Light Light Light

lightolightolighto

light light light

Let there be **light**, and there was light.

L ghtoLightoLighto

Light Light Light

lightolightolighto

light light light

Let there be **light**, and there was light.

For all have sinned, and come short of the **glory** of God.

GloryoGloryoGloryo

Glory Glory Glory

gloryogloryogloryo

glory glory glory

For all have sinned, and come short of the **glory** of God.

GloryoGloryoGloryo

Glory Glory Glory

gloryogloryogloryo

glory glory glory

For all have sinned, and come short of the **glory** of God.

I can do all things through **Christ** which strengtheneth me.

Chr i stoChristoChristo

Christ Christ Christ

chr i stochristochristo

christ christ christ

I can do all things through **Christ** which strengtheneth me.

ChrīstоChristoChristo

Christ Christ Christ

chrīstochristochristo

christ christ christ

I can do all things through **Christ** which strengtheneth me.

I can do all things through **Christ** which strengtheneth me.

Strengthenetho

Strengtheneth

strengthenetho

strengtheneth

I can do all things through **Christ** which strengtheneth me.

Strengthenetho

Strengtheneth

strengthenetho

strengtheneth

I can do all things through **Christ** which strengtheneth me.

But the Lord is **faithful**.

Fa i thf u loFaithfulo

Faithful Faithful

fa i thf u lofaithfulo

faithful faithful

But the Lord is **faithful**.

Fa i thf u loFaithfulo

Faithful Faithful

fa i thf u lofaithfulo

faithful faithful

But the Lord is **faithful**.

Fa i thf u lo Faithful o

Faithful Faithful

fa i thf u lo faithful o

faithful faithful

But the Lord is **faithful**.

Set your **affections** on things above.

AffectionsoAffectionso

Affections Affections

affectionsoaffectionso

affections affections

Set your **affections** on things above.

Affectionso Affectionso

Affections Affections

affectionso affectionso

affections affections

Set your **affections** on things above.

Be **strong** and **courageous**.

StrongoStrongostrongo

Strong strong

Courageo usoCourageouso

Courageous courageous

Be **strong** and **courageous**.

StrongoStrongostrongo

Strong strong

Courageo usoCourageouso

Courageous courageous

Be **strong** and **courageous**.

But I have **trusted** in thy **mercy**.

TrustedoTrustedotrustedo

Trusted trusted

MercyoMercyomercyo

Mercy mercy

But I have **trusted** in thy **mercy**.

TrustedoTrustedotrustedo

Trusted trusted

MercyoMercyomercyo

Mercy mercy

But I have **trusted** in thy **mercy**.

This is the **day** which the **LORD** has made.

Dayodayo Dayodayo

Day day

Lordolordo Lordolordo

Lord lord

This is the **day** which the **LORD** has made.

DayodayoDayodayo

Day day

LordolordoLordolordo

Lord lord

This is the **day** which the **LORD** has made.

The **heavens declare** the glory of God.

HeavensoHeavenso

Heavens heavens

DeclareoDeclareodeclareo

Declare declare

The **heavens declare** the glory of God.

HeavensoHeavenso

Heavens heavens

DeclareoDeclareodeclareo

Declare declare

The **heavens declare** the glory of God.

I am the way and the **truth** and the **life**.

Tr u thotr u thoTruthotrutho

Truth truth

L i feol i feoLifeolifto

Life life

I am the way and the **truth** and the **life**.

Truthotruthotruthotrutho

Truth truth

Lifeolifeolifeolifto

Life life

I am the way and the **truth** and the **life**.

A merry **heart** doeth good like a **medicine**.

HeartoheartoHeartoheartoheartо

Heart heart

MedicineoMedicineo

Medicine medicine

A merry **heart** doeth good like a **medicine**.

HeartoheartoHeartoheartO

Heart heart

Med i c i neoMedicineo

Medicine medicine

A merry **heart** doeth good like a **medicine**.

Faith can **move mountains**.

MoveoMoveomoveo

Move move

MountainsoMountainso

Mountains mountains

Faith can **move mountains**.

MoveoMoveomoveo

Move move

Mountainso Mountainso

Mountains mountains

Faith can **move mountains**.

In **him** I **live** and move and have my being.

H i moh i moHimohimo

Him him

L i veol i veoLiveoliveo

Live live

In **him** I **live** and move and have my being.

H i moh i moHimohimo

Him him

L i veol i veoLiveoliveo

Live live

In **him** I **live** and move and have my being.

I will **walk** by faith even when I **can not see**.

WalkowalkoWalkowalko

Walk walk

canonotoseeocanonotoseeo

can not see

I will **walk** by faith even when I **can not see**.

WalkowalkoWalkowalko

Walk walk

canonotoseeocanonotoseeo

can not see

I will **walk** by faith even when I **can not see**.

In **everything** give **Thanks.**

Everyth i ngoEverythingo

Everything everything

ThanksoThanksothankso

Thanks thanks

In **everything** give **Thanks.**

Everyth i ngoEverythingo

Everything everything

ThanksoThanksothankso

Thanks thanks

In **everything** give **Thanks**.

Seek **peace**, and **pursue** it.

PeaceopeaceoPeaceopeaceo

Peace peace

P*it*rs *it*eoPursueopursueo

Pursue pursue

Seek **peace**, and **pursue** it.

PeaceopeaceoPeaceopeaceo

Peace peace

P[illegible]rs [illegible]eoPursueopursueo

Pursue pursue

Seek **peace**, and **pursue** it.

For we walk by faith, not by sight.

Foroweowalkobyofa th,o
notobyosight.o

For we walk by faith,
not by sight.
For we walk by faith,
not by sight.

For we walk by faith, not by sight.

Foroweowalkobyyofa th,o

notobyyosght.o

For we walk by faith,

not by sight.

For we walk by faith,

not by sight.

Be still, and know that I am God.

Beost il,oandoknowothato
IoamoGod.o

Be still, and know
that I am godd

I am God.

Be still, and know that I am God.

Beostill,oandoknowothato

loamoGod.o

Be still, and know that

I am God.

Be still, and know that

I am God.

The Lord is my shepherd, I shall not want.

TheoLordo isomyoshepherdo

Ioshallonotowant.o

The Lord is my shepherd

I shall not want.

The Lord is my shepherd

I shall not want.

The Lord is my shepherd, I shall not want.

TheoLordo isomyoshepherdo

loshallonotowant.o

The Lord is my shepherd

I shall not want.

The Lord is my shepherd

I shall not want.

For my yoke is easy, and my burden is light.

Foromyoyokeo isoeasy,o

andomyob urdeno isol ight.o

For my yoke is easy,

and my burden is light.

For my yoke is easy,

and my burden is light.

For my yoke is easy, and my burden is light.

Foromyoyokeo soeasy,o
andomyob rdeno sol ght.o

For my yoke is easy,
and my burden is light.
For my yoke is easy,
and my burden is light.

I will joy in the God of my salvation.

low Ilojoyo notheoGodo
ofomyosalvat on.o

I will joy in the God
of my salvation.

I will joy in the God
of my salvation.

I will joy in the God of my salvation.

low Ilojoyo notheoGodo
ofomyosalvat on.o

I will joy in the God
of my salvation.

I will joy in the God
of my salvation.

Let there be light, and there was light.

Letothereobeolight,o
andothereowasolight.o

Let there be light,
and there was light.
Let there be light,
and there was light.

Let there be light, and there was light.

Letothereobeolight,o
andothereowasolight.o

Let there be light,

and there was light.

Let there be light,

and there was light.

But the Lord is faithful.

B totheoLordo sofa thf l.o

B totheoLordo sofa thf l.o

But the Lord is faithful.

But the Lord is faithful.

But the Lord is faithful.

But the Lord is faithful.

But the Lord is faithful.

B totheoLordo sofaithf l.o

B totheoLordo sofaithf l.o

But the Lord is faithful.

But the Lord is faithful.

But the Lord is faithful.

But the Lord is faithful.

Set your affections on things above.

Setoyo roaffect onso

onoth ingsoabove.o

Set your affections

on things above.

Set your affections

on things above.

Set your affections on things above.

Setoyo roaffect onso

onoth ingsoabove.o

Set your affections

on things above.

Set your affections

on things above.

Be strong and courageous.

Beostrongo

andocourageous.o

Be strong

and courageous.

Be strong

and courageous.

Be strong and courageous.

Beostrongo

andocourageous.o

Be strong

and courageous.

Be strong

and courageous.

But I have trusted in thy mercy.

B tolohaveotr stedo

inothyomercy.o

But I have trusted

in thy mercy.

But I have trusted

in thy mercy.

But I have trusted in thy mercy.

B u t o l o have o t r u s t e d o

i n o thy o mercy. o

But I have trusted

in thy mercy.

But I have trusted

in thy mercy.

This is the day which the LORD has made.

Thisoisotheodayowhicho
theoLordohasomade.o

This is the day which
the Lord has made.

This is the day which
the Lord has made.

This is the day which the LORD has made.

Thisoisotheodayowhicho
theoLordohasomade.o

This is the day which
the Lord has made.
This is the day which
the Lord has made.

I am the way and the truth and the life.

loamotheowayoando

theotruthoandotheol ife.o

I am the way and

the truth and the life.

I am the way and

the truth and the life.

I am the way and the truth and the life.

loamotheowayoando

theotruthoandotheol ife.o

I am the way and

the truth and the life.

I am the way and

the truth and the life.

A merry heart doeth good like a medicine.

Aomerryoheartodoetho
goodolikeoaomedicine.o

A merry heart doeth
good like a medicine.

A merry heart doeth
good like a medicine.

A merry heart doeth good like a medicine.

Aomerryoheartodoetho goodolikeoaomedicine.o

A merry heart doeth

good like a medicine.

A merry heart doeth

good like a medicine.

Faith can move mountains.

Fa thocanomoveo

mo nta ns.o

Faith can move

mountains.

Faith can move

mountains.

Faith can move mountains.

Fa thocanomoveo

mo nta ns.o

Faith can move

mountains.

Faith can move

mountains.

In everything give Thanks.

Inoeveryth ngog veo Thanks.o

In everything give Thanks.

In everything give Thanks.

In everything give Thanks.

Inoeveryth ingog iveo
Thanks.o

In everything give
Thanks.

In everything give
Thanks.

The Lord is on my side.

TheoLordo isoonomyos ide.o

TheoLordo isoonomyos ide.o

The Lord is on my side.

The Lord is on my side.

The Lord is on my side.

The Lord is on my side.

The Lord is on my side.

TheoLordo isoonomyos ide.o

TheoLordo isoonomyos ide.o

The Lord is on my side.

The Lord is on my side.

The Lord is on my side.

The Lord is on my side.

We love him, because he first loved us.

Weoloveohim,obecauseo
heofirstolovedous.o

We love him, because
he first loved us.

We love him, because
he first loved us.

We love him, because he first loved us.

Weoloveoh m,obeca seo
heof rstolovedo s.o

We love him, because
he first loved us.
We love him, because
he first loved us.

Seek peace, and pursue it.

Seekopeace,o

andop rs eo to

Seek peace,

and pursue it.

Seek peace,

and pursue it.

Seek peace, and pursue it.

Seekopeace,o

andop us eo to

Seek peace,

and pursue it.

Seek peace,

and pursue it.

www.ingramcontent.com/pod-product-compliance
Lightning Source LLC
LaVergne TN
LVHW060823170826
845678LV00010B/1886

* 9 7 9 8 8 4 8 0 0 6 3 7 7 *